WALKING WITH ANGELS

Inspired Writings
By
Sandra J Yearman

SERAPHIM PUBLISHING LLC

WE WILL BRING LIGHT TO ALL
THE DARK PLACES

Registered trademark-
Sandra J Yearman
Seraphim Publishing
438 Water St. Cambridge, WI 53523

Copyright © 2009 Sandra J Yearman
Produced in the United States of America
Author : Sandra J Yearman
Editor: Sandra J Yearman
Cover Design by Sandra J Yearman
Layout and design by Sandra J Yearman

All rights reserved. No part of this book may be reproduced, stored in or introduced into a retrieval system, or transmitted, in any form or by any means, electronic or mechanical, including photocopying or recording or otherwise copied for public or private use—other than for "fair use" as brief quotations embodied in articles and reviews--without written permission from the author.

Library of Congress Control Number: 2009914156
ISBN: 978-0-9841506-5-6
First Edition

The Lights That Brighten
This World
Are Often Heaven Sent
To Guide Us Through Our
Darkness
As Only God Has Meant
Amen
Amen
Amen

CONTENTS

DEDICATION

Angels Walk Among Us..7
An Angel's Kiss...10
God Is All..13
My Children..15
The Love Of But One..17
Ask The Angels To Guide You......................................19
Walking With Angels..21

SEEKING LIGHT IN THE DARKNESS

Crippled..24
Let Man Remember..27
God Consume Us..30
The Course Of Man..32
God, My Friend Is Dying..36
Time Is A Master..38
What Is Our Purpose..40
In This Time...43
Angry Waves to Toss..45
Satan...47
Lost In The Darkness...49
The Cries Of The Children...51
Politicians And Kings...53

CONTENTS

Reflections..56
Never Forget...59
Man's Reality..62
Disposable Children....................................64
Who Has The Power...................................66
The Battle...68
At The Very End...71
Words Of The Holy Man............................74
Missing Piece..76

COMING HOME

Solo Gloria Deo...79
To Reveal..80
If God Returned To Earth Today...............82
You Do Not Walk Alone............................84
Sampson's Song..86

Dedication

Angels Walk Among Us

Angels walk among us
Save us from disgrace
Protect us from our choices
Your Holy Light to replace

The darkness that defeats us
The sin that weighs us down
The fear and guilt and horror
That would block us from Your Crown

Angels walk among us
And heal us with Your Love
May Your Holy Presence
Bring blessings from above

Angels walk among us
And show us as You see
Break the chains that bind us
And set God's children free

Angels walk among us
In these unholy battle grounds
Save us from the terror
And fill us with the sound

Of the Holiness of Heaven
Of the Song the Angels sing
Of the Voice of our Lord
His Holy Words to bring

Us to the Holy places
The paths we had once tread
We will remember Sacred faces
We will no longer walk among the dead

Amen Amen Amen

An Angel's Kiss

The darkness was overwhelming
Each soldier filled with fear
The red blood flowed like water
We prayed to bring the Heavens near

As I looked upon the battle field
I thought my eyes deceived
As I saw the Angels carry
The souls I was to grieve

And the blood turned into roses
The pain, it fell away
As the Angels carried souls
Off that battle field that day

The horror that surrounded
No longer brought me fear
As I realized the Angels
Meant that God was always near

I saw them bless the many
And cry with anguished pain
At the chaos caused by men
At the bodies that were stained

And the blood turned into roses
The pain, it fell away
As the Angels carried souls
Off that battle field that day

As I watched the Angels
I no longer heard the bullets ring
I heard the music of Heaven
I saw the Angel's wings

As her wings engulfed me
She said I will take you Home
She kissed me on my forehead
And said your sins have been Atoned

And the blood turned into roses
The pain, it fell away
As the Angels carried souls
Off that battle field that day

Amen Amen Amen

God Is All

God is the only Power
Though darkness would disguise
With illusions of grandeur
Terror and lies

God is Almighty
No other takes His place
Our Savior, Redeemer
Our Father filled with Grace

God is all Knowing
No darkness can hide
He Loves His children
With Him should abide

God is all Loving
Creator of Life
Filled with compassion
He saves us from strife

Caught up in the illusions
We may lose our way
Pray to Jesus
His Presence to stay

Amen Amen Amen

My Children

God let them be warriors and healers
Poets and kings
Let them be Angels
Your Holy Will to bring

God let them bring
Your Blessings and Light
Use them to heal
The darkness of the night

Lord let my offspring
Be tools of Your Hand
Use them to save
This world of man

Lord let this life
With its Blessings and Grace
Call out Your Name
And bring Holiness to this place

Amen Amen Amen

The Love Of But One

His eyes were old and clouded
His hair a long time gray
A spirit filled with joy
Who blessed others all his days

The family he came into
Pieces that made a whole
Like the tapestry of God
That sings the Song of the Soul

His life beginnings
Were tainted with torture and pain
But the love he radiated
The life he overcame

Miracles occur in this world
Countless beyond belief
Open up your heart
Truth is the great release

Love transcends all boundaries
His life a tribute to Grace
The love of but one
All darkness can erase

Amen Amen Amen

Ask The Angels To Guide You

Never alone in this world
Will God's children be
If they call out His Name
They will always walk with Thee

Protected by His Power
Surrounded by His Light
He will help us conquer
The darkness of the night

Ask the Angels to guide you
Ask the Angels to stay
Ask the Angels to help you
Conquer the tests that you may

Overcome the darkness
Transcend the barriers of this life
Learn how to love
Dissolve the strife

Amen Amen Amen

Walking With Angels

Walking with Angels
Invisible to see
Their presence is with us
Messengers from Thee

A whisper from Heaven
Miracles to behold
They guide and protect us
As Heaven fore told

Lighting our darkness
Teaching His Song
Instruments of God
Correcting our wrongs

In our hour of darkness
They draw us near
To comfort and guide us
And heal all our fears

And in the silence
Their whispers you will hear
A Heavenly reminder
That God is always near

Amen Amen Amen

Seeking Light In The Darkness

Crippled

Crippled was his spirit
Tortured was his soul
Living in denial
Had taken an earthly toll

Imprisoned by the walls he built
To keep his spirit in
Afraid to experience life
He hid in a world of sin

He longed for freedom
Yet he built the walls that bind
He said he looked for love
Yet darkness was all he could find

God sent him an Angel
She talked to him every day
But his fearful darkness
Made him send the Angel away

He prayed to God to help him
Yet he shunned the gifts God sent
He was as afraid of God
As he was the world of men

God walk with us
Overcome our fears
Help us not to reject you
Bring the Heavens near

Help us to realize
We are the jailors, we sought to flee
Help us to transcend the darkness
And to live our lives with Thee

Amen Amen Amen

Let Man Remember

The world hurled into darkness
As a great man fell
The victorious screams
Emitted from hell

When pride and politics
Have obliterated the Son
And mankind has forgotten
What courage and integrity have won

Lord heal us
Before the darkness takes us all
Let our memories
Be more than man's great fall

When the cowards
Lie in wait
Consumed and spreading
Satan's hate

When the innocents
Are the prey of the dark hand
And fear and hatred
Are embodied in man

God forgive us
And the darkness we create
Cleanse us
From our fear, bigotry and hate

Let man remember
The Songs You sing
Let them surrender their hearts
And allow You in

Amen Amen Amen

God Consume Us

Consume us with Your Love
Fill us with Your Grace
Come and stand before us
In the darkness of this place

Fill us with Your Love
Bless us with Your Grace
Send Your Power and Justice
To eradicate the darkness of this place

Engulf us with Your Love
Immerse us in Your Grace
Help Your children
To seek Your Holy Face

God consume us with Your Love
God fill us with Your Grace
Let this prayer surpass
The boundaries of time and space

Amen Amen Amen

The Course Of Man

The soldiers hidden in the darkness
Shivering from the cold
Filled with fear and terror
Ancient battles of old

A voice rang through the darkness
The sweetness of the Song
Startled the weary soldiers
Stopped the angry throngs

Some say it was an Angle
Some say it was a dream
That stopped that bloody battle
That silenced the horrid screams

A single voice pierced the darkness
A single voice drowned the din
A single voice opened the door
And let God's Spirit in

On that bloody battlefield
The soldiers stopped to stare
At a miracle in their presence
More than they could bear

The voice sang with such sweetness
The Spirit took control
The hearts of men were healed
The conscious soon to know

Glory Alleluia
In excelsis rings
Your Father, God and Savior
His Love and Peace to bring

Some say it was an Angle
Some say it was a dream
That stopped that bloody battle
That silenced the horrid screams

The battlefield was exposed
As a light grew in the sky
Outlining the bodies of the troops
The living and those who had died

The Angels walked among them
Though the soldiers could not see
For they were blinded by the light
Some screamed and some did flee

Some say they felt a presence
Some say they felt a hand
Some say they saw a miracle
That changed the course of man

Amen Amen Amen

God, My Friend Is Dying

God I heard the news today
That one who I hold dear
Is sick and he is dying
I pray You hold him near

Bring comfort to his family
Bring comfort to his being
Carry them when they fall
Let him know his life had meaning

A warrior once he herald
But now that he is old
His memories are fading
In stories he has told

Surround my friends with Angels
Carry him through this strife
Bless the family that remains
Bless his loving wife

Amen Amen Amen

Time Is A Master

Time is a master
No human can defy
No matter how they try to control
They are subject until they die

Who do we allow to be our masters
Who do we choose to obey
Who do we give our power to
On what path do we stay

Time it is unending
But the illusions do betray
Is there more to this existence
Is there a better Way

God help us to transcend our
boundaries
Help us to be free
Of the bondage and the torment
Let us live our lives with Thee

Amen Amen Amen

What Is Our Purpose

Why are we here
Is it fate or more
Coincidence
Or the Holy Door

What are our missions
What are the tests
Can we conquer the darkness
And walk with the blessed

When do we question
When do we seek
Do we challenge the darkness
Or hide with deceit

Lord I pray to Thee
Help us to see
The reasons we are here
The missions of Thee

Help us to hear You
To see as You see
To understand our creation
The blessings of Thee

Help us to rise above
The darkness and disgrace
Forgive us for calling to demons
And destroying the Holy places

Help us to remember
Help us to See
Help us to Awaken
And return Home to Thee

Amen Amen Amen

In This Time

The journeys I have taken
In this earthly life
At times I have felt blessed
At times crippled by my strife

I try to see each journey
As an adventure sent by Thee
Tests that I must take
Mirrors that I must see

I have seen many wonders
I have seen horror beyond my years
I have tasted great delights
I have conquered many fears

I have seen love in the night sky
I have heard Angels whisper in
the wind
I have seen the Hand of God
I know from where I begin

The journeys I have taken
The travels I have been
I would not change one minute
I would do them all again

For every test that I have conquered
And every mountain I have climbed
Has brought me to this place
Has put me in this time

Amen Amen Amen

Angry Waves To Toss

The pipes play in the distance
Another comrade lost
Drowned in the dark oceans
Angry waves to toss

The Spirit is unyielding
The flesh is lost at sea
The warrior's task unending
In death he cries to Thee

What then is the journey
Another life is lost
What is the meaning
What answers are sought

Drowning in our darkness
Yet, to flee the pain
What is mankind's mask
What is he to gain

Lord, Your children are sinking
In the darkness here
Please save and forgive them
Bring Your Presence here

Amen Amen Amen

Satan

Satan in his ignorance
Sought to take a stand
In defiance of God
To consume the world of man

But blinded with his hatred
His ignorance and fear
He failed to hear the Song of God
When holy children called God near

Readying his armies
The depths of darkness known
They sought to conquer creation
To reap the seeds that they had sown

Focused on the victims
He failed to see the Light
Rising from the East
Consuming all the night

His ego had betrayed him
He over played his might
He never had the power
To overcome the Light

Amen Amen Amen

Lost In The Darkness

He was lost in the chaos
They never saw him go
The horror destroyed his spirit
The man, no longer to know

Wars of all the ages
The consequences of hell
The tolls inconceivable
Bodies turned to shells

The spirit shrank in the vessel
The body could not take hold
When the being sank in darkness
The man, no longer to know

He never heard the bullet
He never saw the stone
He never heard his soul die
He never made it home

God forgive Your creations
Save us from our hells
Bless us with Your Presence
Bring us Home to dwell

Amen Amen Amen

The Cries Of The Children

He sold her to a monster
Their family needed bread
She was powerless
She had no choice to wed

The cries of the children through
the ages
Some are loved and some are lost
The forgotten and the nameless
The chosen and the bought

The years turn to centuries
Yet man's behavior stays the same
Will we ever transcend our darkness
In humanity's hellacious games

The cries of the children through
the ages
Some are loved and some are lost
The forgotten and the nameless
The chosen and the bought

In this world of madness
The heartache and the greed
God we need You more than ever
Your children need You to lead

Us out of the mazes we are trapped in
Out of the dark walls that we build
We need Your Love and Forgiveness
Your Holy Sword to wield

Amen Amen Amen

Politicians And Kings

They wanted to be soldiers
Politicians and kings
They were never prepared
For what the darkness of man
can bring

When horror becomes routine
And we no longer listen to the screams
in the night
What does this say about humanity
What does this say about man's plight

Can one still have honor
In the world of the dead
Can integrity exist
Unless the death masks are shed

They wanted to be soldiers
Politicians and kings
They were never prepared
For what the darkness of man
can bring

They fought for freedom
Then the leaders betrayed
Where blood was shed
Where bodies were laid

Man dreams of power
To hold and control
Some pray to God
Others lose their souls

What is the price
To fulfill our needs
To glorify our bodies
To justify our deeds

God in Your Mercy
Help us to see
The only power
Lies in Thee

God give us Faith
Truth and Might
So we can conquer
The demons in the night

Amen Amen Amen

Reflections

Reflections of the fallen
Whose images do we see
Faces of the victims
Are they reflections of you and me

Quiet in the chaos
Fear within the storm
Anarchy in the garden
The worlds in which we are born

God give us a Light to follow
A Voice to guide us through the night
Save us from our madness
Protect us with Your Might

Guide us through the illusions
That the reflections we may recognize
As the Holiness from Heaven
Breaking through the human guise

Amen Amen Amen

Never Forget

Never forget
Are the words they said
To remind the world
To honor the dead

Never forget
When darkness took control
When fear and hatred
Played a significant role

Never forget
The victims, the lost
The insanity
The demons sought

Through nights of terror
Through days of fear
Their faith and their courage
Through all those long years

God we have seen horror
Hatred and sin
It is man calling to darkness
The demons, they let in

Lord, never forget
Your children here
Protect them and bless them
Please hold them near

Lord, through the ages
Mistakes we have made
We have opened the graves
With demons have lain

Please forgive us
For our ignorance and fear
Help us to overcome our darkness
I call the Heavens near

Lord, You have many children
They call You by many Names
You are our Father
The One and the Same

Please walk among us
Help us to heal
Open our hearts
To You we would kneel

Help us remember
The Love, we thought lost
Our Home in the Heavens
Our Salvation You bought

Lord, walk among us
Let it be Your Voice that we hear
I call to the Heavens
Your Presence we feel

Amen Amen Amen

Man's Reality

We sleep to escape the madness
Then our nightmares turn to pain
And we are brought back into the darkness
Of man's reality again

The screams we hear in our slumber
Are our own voices, we do not recognize
Are dreams just an extension
Of our earthly guise

Man creates illusions
Both awake and asleep
He strives to control realities
A force he cannot keep

Why does man create illusions
When God, perfect gifts does send
Is it to justify darkness
Or to hide from the fear that has no end

God help us to realize
That it is You, who gives us what we need
It is Your reality we should strive for
Forgive us for our deeds

Engulf us with Your Holy Light
Open our eyes that we may see
The reality of Your world
The world where we are free

Amen Amen Amen

Disposable Children

Nightmares in the walking
Hopelessness abounds
Deafening are the cries
Horror in the sounds

Life so young and ageless
Shortened by a choice
Victims on the streets
Cries without a voice

Where do they run to
To whom do they call
Motivated by fears
The tragedy of all

God bless Your children
Both here and afar
Protect them from darkness
Reassemble the shards

God hear the cries
Of the lost and alone
The victims, the predators
With Your Love Atone

Disposable children
The hells we create
God stand before them
And save them from their chosen fate

Amen Amen Amen

Who Has The Power

We create our illusions
By our perceptions and our fears
Our realities are altered
By the voices that we hear

The instruments of creation
The minds of man
Influence our realities
Slaves to man's hands

Running through the illusions
Filled with fear
Father save Your children
We call Your Presence here

Forgive us for our ignorance
Our vanity and our greed
Replace our darkness
With Your Holy Creed

Help us to overcome
Our need to hate
Our violence, our egos
Save us from our fates

God we need Your Presence
Your Forgiveness to cleanse
Your Love to heal
Your Angels to send

Amen Amen Amen

The Battle

The children were frightened
There was terror in the land
The demons they called to
Were taking their price on demand

The children had been seduced
With glistening gold
With stories of power
Their souls were sold

They opened the doors
And invited the demons in
They traded their lives
For bondage and sin

They led the demons
To their Holy places
In servitude and payment
The children hid the traces

Of the Holiness within them
Of their Love and Grace
They sold it all
For the darkness of this place

But God was watching
He never turns away
He sent a Savior
Their sentences to stay

Into the temple
Entered the Light
Faced the master of darkness
Looked into the face of terror and fright

The demons trembled
As they were blinded by the Holy Light
They attacked and they screamed
And they fought with their might

But the Light of Heaven
Conquered the disgrace
And He brought God's Light
Back into this place

Amen Amen Amen

At The Very End

Little was her time here
Is what the doctors said
Confused and anxious
About the life she led

Was her fear, for staying here
Or fear for going Home
She had always felt so lost
In this world to roam

She never felt satisfied
With any of the choices she made
There were so many people in her life
But none of them ever stayed

How frail was her existence
How fragile was her life
Always filled with darkness
Anger, jealousy and strife

At what point do you let God in
Do you finally listen to His Voice
Do you lay your fear aside
Do you make the Holy choice

Angels were always with her
But she refused to see
That God Loved her as His child
That there was more to this world than she could see

The last time that I saw her
She was taking a journey with a friend
She finally found her Peace
At the very end

Amen Amen Amen

Words Of The Holy Man

That they should seek God
The Holy man said
Of all the men God created
The purpose of the undead

In the hope they might find Him
In the hope they would be saved
In the hope of the Anointed
Who conquered the grave

In the hope they might feel of Him
His Presence to sense
His Voice to hear
His Light to conquer the dense

Darkness we hide in
Darkness we wear
Darkness that calls us
Allegiance we swear

God, let the Prophet's
Words ring true
Let men conquer their darkness
And seek only You

God bless us with Your Presence
Bless us with Your Grace
Protect us and save us
From the darkness we face

Amen Amen Amen

Missing Peace

Her missing piece
Made her cry
Made her call out to the Heavens
Made her question why

Her life, an arduous journey
Was filled with thrills and fear
Filled with triumphs and failures
As others, she held dear

Something always seemed missing
The piece that she sought
She took many paths
Many battles she fought

Through her life's journey
Answers she would seek
To understand
The missing piece

She came full circle
She Awakened in this life
She conquered the darkness
She transcended the strife

And in her wisdom
The piece she had sought
Was the Peace of God
Of which Jesus had taught

Amen Amen Amen

Coming Home

Solo Gloria Deo

To God alone give Glory
To God alone give Praise
The Father and the Author
The Son from death did raise

Laus Deo
Praise to God be given
Sing the voices of the Angels
To earth and all of Heaven

Domine Deus, Rex caelestis
O Lord God, Heavenly King
We beg Your forgiveness
And Your praises we sing

Adoramus te, Adoramus te

Amen Amen Amen

To Reveal

Fear not, said the Lord
I AM the First and the Last
I AM the Future
I AM the Past

There are no others before Me
I AM who I AM
I AM your God and Father
I AM the Holy Lamb

And I will reveal to you
The Secretes of the Song
The Holiness of Heaven
The corrections of what is wrong

Take up your bed and follow
Believe in me as a child
I will never leave you
All your years, all your whiles

Amen Amen Amen

If God Returned
To Earth Today

If God returned to earth today
How would He be received
Would He be recognized
By those who profess to believe

Would we know Him
Would we let Him in
Or would we hide in horror
Because of our ghastly sin

Would He be honored
Or heckled as of old
Would we learn from our mistakes
As the Bible has told

Would we invite Him to dwell with us
Would we feed Him at our table
Would we give Him clothes and rest
And provide as we are able

Would we take His Hand
And leave all we have owned
Or would we put more value
On the trinkets that we own

God is always with us
We answer these questions each day
He sends His Light from Heaven
To show us the Holy Way

Amen Amen Amen

You Do Not Walk Alone

You do not walk alone
Take comfort in these words
The message that God sends
The Song the Angels herald

God is always with us
His Angels He does send
The messengers of Heaven
Our guardians and our friends

In these worlds of peril
Terror and grief
Call out to the Lord
He will send you great relief

Ask Him to send you Angels
To guard you in the night
For God will always listen
And protect you with His Might

God will never leave you
Call out His Name
His Love is Eternal
His Blessings of the same

You do not walk alone
Take comfort in these words
The message that God sends
The Song the Angels herald

Amen Amen Amen

Sampson's Song

I will not leave you on this journey
You will know my Love and more
And when your time has ended
I will walk you to Heaven's door

I have been with you forever
Our Love has made us soar
And when the journey is over
I will walk you to Heaven's door

Our Love transcends all boundaries
A covenant that we swore
When the days are over
I will walk you to Heaven's door

Amen Amen Amen

Never Alone In This World
Will God's Children Be
If They Call Out His Name
They Will Always Walk With Thee
Amen
Amen
Amen

www.ingramcontent.com/pod-product-compliance
Lightning Source LLC
Chambersburg PA
CBHW051709040426
42446CB00008B/800